CONVERGE
Bible Studies

CRIES OF THE POOR

CONVERGE
Bible Studies

CRIES OF THE POOR

GRACE BISKIE

Abingdon Press
Nashville

CRIES OF THE POOR
CONVERGE BIBLE STUDIES

By Grace Biskie

Copyright © 2014 by Abingdon Press

Library of Congress Cataloging-in-Publication Data has been requested.

ISBN: 978-1-4267-9555-8

Series Editor: Shane Raynor

14 15 16 17 18 19 20 21 22 23—10 9 8 7 6 5 4 3 2 1

Manufactured in the United States of America

CONTENTS

ABOUT THE SERIES

Converge is a series of topical Bible studies based on the Common English Bible translation. Each title in the *Converge* series consists of four studies based around a common topic or theme. *Converge* brings together a unique group of writers from different backgrounds, traditions, and age groups.

HOW TO USE THESE STUDIES

Converge Bible studies can be used by small groups, classes, or individuals. Each study uses a simple format. For the convenience of the reader, the primary Scripture passages are included. In Insight and Ideas, the author of the study explores each Scripture passage, going deeper into the text and helping readers understand how the Scripture connects with the theme of the study. Questions are designed to encourage both personal reflection and group conversation. Some questions may not have simple answers. That's part of what makes studying the Bible so exciting.

Although Bible passages are included with each session, study participants may find it useful to have personal Bibles on hand for referencing other Scriptures. *Converge* studies are designed for use with the Common English Bible; but they work well with any modern, reliable translation.

ONLINE EXTRAS

Converge studies are available in both print and digital formats. Each title in the series has additional components that are available online, including related blog posts and podcasts.

To access the companion materials, visit

http://www.MinistryMatters.com/Converge

Thanks for using *Converge*!

INTRODUCTION

I told my editor, Shane, that I'd love to write a study called *Cries of the Poor* at a time when I was sitting fairly comfortably in a great job without any major drama to speak of. Interestingly enough, at the time of this writing, my job is gone and I myself am poor. *Womp, womp, womp.* Essentially, I made myself a case study.

I can't say that it's been easy to ask others for help, to find myself here, and to look to the government for assistance. Yet there is something a bit more genuine when writing about God's love for the poor while one is experiencing it. For that reason, I'm glad to be going through this. These words have been a balm for my soul and a reminder of how God loves me and sees me—broke as a joke. The passages from 1 John 3; Matthew 5 and 25; and Isaiah 58 knocked me upside my head about 35 times with the absolute reality of God's concern for the cries of the poor. Strangely enough, God has taken great interest in using us to care for the poor. We've been given a heavy responsibility to make a difference. God gives us incentive and direction, rewards and benefits; but ultimately the onus is on us. Us.

As we'll see from the passage in Isaiah 58, God wants to use our generosity to care for the poor to also transform our hearts. I understand the tension here. We don't want to serve the poor for the reward, making us selfish and every bit as narcissistic as a Pharisee. Yet we see God offering rewards for "good behavior," and the rewards sound pretty darn good. Isaiah 58:8 offers a few blessings for those aligned with God: "Then your light will break out like the dawn, and you will be healed quickly. Your own righteousness will walk before you, and the LORD's glory will be your rear guard."

Who wouldn't want the glory of the Lord to be their rear guard? Who would tell the Lord, "Thanks but no thanks, God. I'm all filled up on light, quick healing, guidance, protection and presence. I'm good, Lord, but thanks! Good lookin' out!"

So then how do we proceed? How do we enact justice and distribute benevolence, without a little hope that our light is going to break out like the dawn? The answer is fairly simple, actually.

When we focus on ourselves, the result is usually disastrous. And when that happens, we've likely lost our focus on Christ. And sometimes the best way to refocus on Christ is to focus on those Christ loves who are in need.

I wish that it were an easy, 10-step program; but really it's a constant give and take, back and forth. Do it simultaneously—serve the poor; give money; say no to injustice; and watch as God gifts you with humility, healing, and restoration along the way. God said that the people's right behavior would cause the rear guards to provide protection. Part of what the rear guards are is divine protection against all of the things we loathe about ourselves: selfishness, narcissism, and life-sucking self-pity. Repentant people are surrounded by protection against these things. Through our obedience in justice and mercy, God promises to bless us with healing, spiritual restoration, high standards, and even protection from trouble. In Isaiah 58:9, additional promises are made: "Then you will call, and the LORD will answer; you will cry for help, and God will say, 'I'm here.' If you remove the yoke from among you, the finger-pointing, the wicked speech." Please note the word *if*. There is a beautiful give and take, revealing the relational aspects to our interactions with God. Yes, we do this; God does that.

I don't exactly love that particular theology. It makes me feel like a real sleazeball every time. However, if my God desires that I demonstrate my devotion by alleviating hunger and ministering to those who extremely afflicted, then I will do it. And when I have, not only have I received a tremendous sense of joy, peace, hope, and love within my heart, but I've cherished the responses of those who were on the receiving end. What a blessing! Isaiah 58:11-12 says: *"The LORD will guide you continually and provide for you, even in parched places. He will rescue your bones. You will* be like a watered garden, like a spring of water that won't run dry. They will rebuild ancient ruins on your account; the foundations of generations past you will restore. You will be called Mender of Broken Walls, Restorer of Livable Streets" (emphasis mine).

Most of us have never been called "Mender of Broken Walls" or "Restorer of Livable Streets"; but most of us have had another—perhaps a son or daughter, a mentee, a younger sibling—express his or her allegiance to us. Multiply that times a thousand. The blessing of helping others (a family, a city, or a whole community) overcome ruin and destruction in their lives is possible through God's people acting in compassion; and let me tell you, it is *awesome*. Even though we humans have managed to jack everything up, God is greater still to restore and repair. Imagine being called the "repairer of the breach," the "restorer of the streets," where children once went hungry. Imagine. It's a beautifully transformative image. God will use little, old us to restore and repair that which has been decimated. There is so much hope here!

A deep relationship with our Lord can make a real difference in human relationships, especially in our relationship to one another and to money. Know that God is willing to help us put down our selfish behaviors and open our hearts to the cries of the poor in ways that we have never even anticipated. Please take God's hand of transformative grace, clutch it tightly, hold your breath, and get ready to fly.

Blessings to you, "repairer of the breach." Blessings.

1

GOING BEYOND WORDS
LOVING WITH ACTION AND TRUTH

SCRIPTURE
1 JOHN 3:13-24

[13]Don't be surprised, brothers and sisters, if the world hates you. [14]We know that we have transferred from death to life, because we love the brothers and sisters. The person who does not love remains in death. [15]Everyone who hates a brother or sister is a murderer, and you know that no murderer has eternal life residing in him. [16]This is how we know love: Jesus laid down his life for us, and we ought to lay down our lives for our brothers and sisters. [17]But if a person has material possessions and sees a brother or sister in need and that person doesn't care—how can the love of God remain in him?

[18]Little children, let's not love with words or speech but with action and truth. [19]This is how we will know that we belong to the truth and reassure our hearts in God's presence. [20]Even if our

hearts condemn us, God is greater than our hearts and knows all things. [21]Dear friends, if our hearts don't condemn us, we have confidence in relationship to God. [22]We receive whatever we ask from him because we keep his commandments and do what pleases him. [23]This is his commandment, that we believe in the name of his Son, Jesus Christ, and love each other as he commanded us. [24]The person who keeps his commandments remains in God and God remains in him; and this is how we know that he remains in us, because of the Spirit that he has given to us.

INSIGHT AND IDEAS

At first glance this passage might read like a love-fest to-do list in order to obtain new life. Let's get that theory out of the way. The truth is, when we love one another, especially the poor, it is evidence of love for the Father. Every action reveals who and what we are committed to. Yet this passage speaks of something bigger than an every-now-and-then type of love. John's words are bigger and deeper than our usual "follow your heart" clichés. This is a high-calling type of love. High-calling love looks for the good of the beloved at every moment.

Man, that sure is hard to do! We humans are miserably fallen, each of us sin-filled to our core. Our propensity toward sacrificial, high-calling love is almost nil. Sure, we can love and bond with our parents, our deepest friends, and our children; but can we daily, weekly, or even monthly *consistently put others' needs in front of our own* in sacrifice and humility? Surely an ability to do so says something about the type of growth happening in our heart. It's that high-calling love which shines brightest as we care for those with far greater needs than we have.

A TALE OF TWO COMMUNITIES

I was raised among the urban poor in Detroit. For a few years, the house directly across the street was a crack house. I distinctly remember seeing strewn about their lawn the remnants of hard living: liquor bottles in brown paper bags, used condoms, and all manner of disgusting trash. In an effort to keep me from a hard life, my Ma forked over a great deal of her income to send me to a private Christian school where most of the kids lived in cookie-cutter suburbs, complete with manicured lawns and *actual* white picket fences. When I'd visit my suburban friends, the cleanliness of their neighborhoods was jarring. It took my breath away. But excitement over the picture of wealth became a quick reality check when I realized that none of all that clean and seemingly stable goodness was coming over to my hood anytime soon.

Even as a little kid, I knew that it was not supposed to be that way. I knew that systemic inequities lead to these differences, and I knew that no one cared. My Christian school was part of a large church where elders of the church sat on the board for the school. What I knew from my time in the school and as a member of the church was that no one cared about the poorer members of our community. Justice and poverty weren't ever talked about from the pulpit; and when they were addressed in front of me, it came in the form of judgment and racism. I knew that my leaders, teachers, and spiritual mentors actively loathed Detroit and did all they could to avoid it. This left a profound impact on me. One of my core beliefs growing up was that God and his people hated Detroit and all its black residents. In hindsight, I believe that what I noticed was simply indifference at best, prejudice at worst. Either way, the attitude of this suburban church toward my hometown was not love—that much I knew then and that much I know now.

LOVE AND HATE

The opposite of high-calling love isn't merely indifference. Oh, that it was, life would be simpler! No, the opposite of high-calling love is hate. As 1 John 3:15 points out, "Everyone who hates a brother or sister is a murderer, and you know that no murderer has eternal life residing in him." That is not to say that if you do not love, you are not a true believer. The passage simply reminds us that failing to love others through our actions is equal to active hatred. Jesus, who sacrificed all that he had to literal death, gave us the picture of fully living into high-calling love. Jesus was not merely a martyr of the faith, he willingly, sacrificially walked *toward* death on our behalf; there was no hate in him. When we live toward high-calling love, we are actively working to push hate out of our hearts.

Hatred and murder are on the same level because all hatred is a heart issue. Are both the hater and the murderer equally guilty? Yes, both the weight and guilt of our hatred and murders lie more in our motives than our actions.

Therefore, our love or lack of love for the poor is tethered to our motives. Without sacrificial, high-calling love, we are in active hatred toward them. Ouch!

LIVING IN OBEDIENCE

Let's get this straight: To live in obedience to Christ, we have two options: 1) Actively, sacrificially pursue high-calling love to each person, regardless of race, culture, neighborhood, BMW, or beater. 2) Live in active, privileged, disobedient ignorance, which directly affects the welfare of others whom we are called to care about. No pressure or anything, but Jesus' model reveals that we ought to love the poor at all costs—even to death.

It's easy to pass off Christ's life-altering sacrifice on the cross as if it's something we could never do. Yet in this passage, John shows us how to live out that same high-calling love in a real and practical way: Love the poor. Verse 16 states that we ought to lay down our lives for our brothers and sisters. Not that we *must* lay down our lives as if we are forced to; but like Jesus, we walk straight into it. We gird up and let our willingness shine bright like a diamond.

Laying down one's life is no small order, which makes sense when you consider how complex and complicated it can be to integrate a love for the poor into one's everyday life. John stated it this way to make his point loud and clear: You don't need to die on a cross to show your devotion to the cross, but you are expected to self-sacrifice on behalf of others—even if it's unto death.

But forget death, how about just a smidge of awareness? How about being able to acknowledge our brothers and sisters in need without looking away? In verse 17, John states, "But if a person has material possessions and sees a brother or sister in need and that person doesn't care—how can the love of God remain in him?" John's hypothetical Joe has the means to provide. Joe may not be wealthy, but he has at least enough to provide for his less fortunate buddy. One need not be wealthy to give. American Christians live amongst the top 10 percent of the world's wealthiest people. When even our poorest poor have far greater wealth than the rest of the world, we'd be hard pressed to admit to anything else than being a part of humanity's wealthiest elite.

ENGAGING, KNOWING, AND CARING

Let's pause right here to acknowledge that most of us aren't completely heartless when it comes to our indifference to the poor. Oftentimes, we don't care because we don't know. We don't know because we're too overwhelmed. We're too overwhelmed because we've never allowed ourselves to fully engage the poor, let alone sacrifice our lives for them. Engagement here looks a lot less like writing million-dollar checks and more like sacrificially giving a missionary $25 or $50 a month. The challenge for us is to *engage enough* to know and *know enough* to care. We are simply not allowed to see someone in need, know that we can meet the need, and choose our own desires over our less fortunate brothers and sisters. In the absence of high-calling love, there is active hatred. What is erected between the two is now a barrier, which creates relationship poverty. Given these truths, it's easy to see how difficult it is for the wealthy and the poor to live amongst one another when ongoing ignored needs and indifference create relational poverty in two seconds flat. Jesus tells us that when we love the Lord our God, it is tethered to loving our neighbor. This is why John tells us we "ought to" lay down our lives (verse 16). If we don't, we call into question everything that we say is true about our faith.

When John asks how the love of God can remain in our hypothetical Joe, he wants us, the readers, to evaluate for ourselves: What do *you* think about this Joe? Does Joe get the final rose or no? Is the love of God remaining in Joe? The answer to that begs the question, does the love of God remain in you? The way to love the poor is not with our words, John states in verse 18, but with action and truth. This, he says, is how we will know we belong to the truth and reassure our hearts in God's presence.

John prefaces this thought by calling his readers "little children." As a spiritual father, he wanted to appeal to his relational capital and allow himself to be included in this challenge in writing: "Let's"—*let us*—love the poor. *Us.* Let *us* love the poor. But let us not love merely with words; let our love be expressed. Let it show! Our love for the poor should show. Don't go boasting like a banshee about all the good deeds you did for the poor; let it show in your bank account, in your sacrifice.

Because God shows love for us, you ought to, too.

QUESTIONS

1. Who is "the world" in 1 John 3:13? Why does John have an expectation that the world will hate believers?

2. What shows that we have transferred from death to life? How do we respond to another professing believer who doesn't seem to be doing this? What happens if *we* aren't doing this?

3. Is this passage equating hate with murder? Explain why you think it is or it isn't.

4. What does it mean to "lay down our lives" (1 John 3:16)? How much should we be willing to sacrifice for someone else?

5. How does 1 John 3:17 challenge wealthy believers? What about middle-class believers? poor believers in a wealthy society?

6. Why is it important to love with both action and truth? What does it look like if either of these components is left out of the equation?

7. How is 1 John 3:20 reassuring? Why might some people find it unsettling or disquieting?

8. What are the conditions for the outcome in 1 John 3:22? What implications does this have for prayer?

9. What does it mean to remain in God and for God to remain in us (1 John 3:24)? How do we make sure that this happens?

10. How does the Holy Spirit help us love other believers?

11. What are some ways we can individually engage people of other socioeconomic groups and get help for the people who need it most? What are ways we can engage people as a body of believers?

2

HOPELESS AND HAPPY
FACING SPIRITUAL POVERTY

Full in the Lord and you are depending on God!

SCRIPTURE
MATTHEW 5:1-16

[1]Now when Jesus saw the crowds, he went up a mountain. He sat down and his disciples came to him. [2]He taught them, saying:

[3]"Happy are people who are hopeless, because the kingdom of heaven is theirs.

[4]"Happy are people who grieve, because they will be made glad.

[5]"Happy are people who are humble, because they will inherit the earth.

[6]"Happy are people who are hungry and thirsty for righteousness, because they will be fed until they are full.

[7]"Happy are people who show mercy, because they will receive mercy.

[8]"Happy are people who have pure hearts, because they will see God.

[9]"Happy are people who make peace, because they will be called God's children.

[10]"Happy are people whose lives are harassed because they are righteous, because the kingdom of heaven is theirs.

[11]"Happy are you when people insult you and harass you and speak all kinds of bad and false things about you, all because of me. [12]Be full of joy and be glad, because you have a great reward in heaven. In the same way, people harassed the prophets who came before you.

[13]"You are the salt of the earth. But if salt loses its saltiness, how will it become salty again? It's good for nothing except to be thrown away and trampled under people's feet. [14]You are the light of the world. A city on top of a hill can't be hidden. [15]Neither do people light a lamp and put it under a basket. Instead, they put it on top of a lampstand, and it shines on all who are in the house. [16]In the same way, let your light shine before people, so they can see the good things you do and praise your Father who is in heaven.

INSIGHT AND IDEAS

In Matthew 5:3, the following scandalous claim is made: "Happy are people who are hopeless." (*Cue record skipping noise.*) *Jesus, what on earth are you talking about?* Surely

Jesus isn't asking us to pursue poverty. No child says, "Hey, Ma, when I grow up, I can't wait to be hopeless, because Jesus said so!" This passage begs the question: Why would Jesus consider hopelessness a desirable condition?

Hopelessness is a form of poverty. To be clear, temporary hopelessness is not a lack of faith nor spiritual depth; it's a mind-set. It is a natural response to awful circumstances. But we can't live there. We can't set up shop. We can't store up an unhealthy mind-set to keep for convenient use later. However, we *should* store up our treasure of hope in heaven. It's our spiritual blessings after all that will outweigh and outlast any meager thing we can attempt to store up on earth.

FACING OUR MORAL POVERTY

The poverty of hopelessness this passage speaks of, in which Jesus posits will make us happy, is more fully descriptive in the concept of humility. When we allow ourselves to be self-reliant, self-satisfied, and prideful, we have very little understanding of our own weaknesses. At the end of the day, each of us must face our moral poverty. We must face our complete and utter total disregard for others and even ourselves as displayed so meticulously in a three month old. Three-month-old babies "think" only of themselves yet profoundly (and loudly) display their understanding of their dependency on their caregivers. It is with an acknowledgement of our condition that we can come to God in humility, with our hopelessness fully on display— just like the high-pitched three month old. I hate to admit

25

this, but I am happier when my full reliance is in God even when I've had very little and lost much. It's a scary truth. The kind you want to push to the nether regions of your cerebral cortex while you beg God that you'll never have to experience anything like it again or for the first time.

We cannot deny that hopelessness is also born from the adversity of financial poverty, which is all bound up with our self-esteem, self-worth, and emotional stability. When considering the cries of the poor, I'd like to reflect a bit more on poverty itself.

WHEN POVERTY IS AN IDENTITY

In Scripture, poverty often has a possessive pronoun attached to it. It is "their" poverty in Proverbs 10:15 and 31:7, "her" poverty in Mark 12:44 and Luke 21:4, and "their" poverty in 2 Corinthians 8:2. The descriptors indicate ownership.

The power of believing self-inundated lies is shown most powerfully in the poor. My poverty is *mine. This is who I am. I am the sum of my poverty*—all lies. When the focus is inward, a web of negativity ensues. The ability to look to God crumbles along with our shaky sense of self-worth.

Exacerbating the problems of the poor are the not-so-poor folk who make the poor feel as though they're not worthy of God's richest blessings. If you catch yourself making a character judgment on the poor, stop it. Just stop it! When we allow ourselves to internalize these lies, we heap onto the poor the idea that they are a "nobody."

Who is the poor? everyone? But No one!

The poor need your scary looks and unhelpful judgments like they need a hole in their head. Again, stop it! They not only *feel* overlooked, ignored, and irrelevant, they *become* overlooked, ignored, and irrelevant. When that becomes reality to a person and in a society at large, there is irreconcilable self-condemnation. The message of poverty moves from "there is never enough" to "there is never enough *for me,* because I am not worth it." And so the poor are attacked at the deepest level of their identity, value, and purpose; their level of powerlessness is astonishing.

Like Solomon Northup, a former slave on whom the popular film *12 Years a Slave* was based, felt no power because systemic forces kept him enslaved and trapped. The times when the poor should fight are when they settle. The times when they should resolve to take appropriate action are when they lie down, even when it affects their emotional and physical health. The poor are often gripped with repetitive, negative thinking, looking for a glimmer of light but trapped in a dungeon surrounded by thick, impenetrable darkness.

Why did you answer?

That is the weight of poverty. Poverty is a heavy, life-altering, debilitating human condition. The poor will carry shame, guilt, and hopelessness every single day, never believing that they are worthy of anything more than their current condition until Jesus comes along and says, "Hey there, kiddo, I've got something else for you and it's not here on earth." There's the hope in this passage (finally!). It's the hope beyond the current circumstances. Happy are the hopeless, Jesus says, because the kingdom of heaven is *theirs. If the poverty is theirs, so is the kingdom of heaven.* The kingdom of heaven belongs to the poor. It belongs to the humble. It belongs to the hopeless. It belongs to the poor because the deeper wounds of poverty harbor in one's soul and fixate on core identity and purpose. *Poverty isn't merely a financial or situational issue; it is a soul-and-spirit issue.* Jesus addresses this soul-and-spirit issue with a soul-and-spirit answer. Happy are the hopeless because they have an eternal soul-and-spirit home.

WHEN POVERTY IS A MIND-SET

When I was a kid, poverty was the pervading demon that haunted my reality. All of my expectations for myself were given through the framework of poverty. For example, can *someone like me,* a poor little black girl from inner city Detroit, get a college degree? Because poverty had defined my expectations, I did not believe that a bachelor's degree was possible for *someone like me.* Poverty became my Maps app. My poverty mind-set laid out the geography of my life's timeline, showing me which routes were available for *someone like me.* And those routes were few. I assumed that post high-school, I'd find man to become my "baby daddy" of three-ish misbehaved miscreants. Nowhere in the equation was what actually happened: a bachelor's, a master's, years of fruitful ministry, speaking, and writing. These paths were such a wild anomaly that I'd never even considered them—never. If I'd ever considered an alternative path, the weight of lack, doubt, insecurity, and loss revealed the journey to be too scary for *someone like me* to venture out on. In fact, the mind-set pervaded my weary brain until I was 34 years old. I was fearful to begin a seminary program because of where I was from—and what business does *someone like me* have trying to obtain a voice for the kingdom of God? Working through a poverty mind-set in my mid-thirties was humbling, to say the least. Truthfully? It still catches up to me now and then. I have to rehearse Jesus' precious truths, sometimes again and again.

Yet I'm still an American. I haven't been *actually* poor since my early 20s. When I consider the lives of the modern-day *actual* poor and the *actual* hopeless, a wave of fear washes over me for them. Did Jesus really mean that? Did he mean it for the more than two hundred Nigerian girls who were kidnapped into sex slavery, impoverished to begin with? How could they *possibly* cultivate an emotion similar to happiness? It is scandalous. Those girls, the ones who fall victim to hopelessness will not feel happy, they will not feel "blessed and highly favored." The only respite for those in captivity is the hope that the kingdom of heaven is theirs. The irreconcilable connections between poverty, hopelessness, and despair are not easily broken. They move in tandem, like risky toddlers following one another even when the location leads to a messy end.

GOD IS WITH US

When I've been most hopeless, it was downright difficult to even put my feet on the ground in the morning. After losing my father, a job, and a few friends, I've wrestled my inner demons of despair until my knuckles turned white and I walked away with a bloody limp. The poverty of hopelessness in my life has manifested in failure, laziness, agony, compromise, and all manner of unattractive traits. As an abuse survivor who grew up in poverty, I have struggled to set down my victim mentality, to own up to the choices I can make and the decisions I can control.

Yet I haven't quite figured out how to completely toss out hopelessness. When it's on me heavy, it's an emotional jail cell. It's powerlessness embodied in a sobbing woman holding herself in dark corner of the dining room. There were times I understood my inner and external resources available to me, yet I floundered in my hopelessness—at times even considering suicide.

I was 22 when my Ma suffered severe health problems that left her a shell of her former self, buried in debt, and unable to care for herself. I struggled as a relatively new believer to reconcile hope with the reality of our situation. One day, as foreclosure was bearing down on us, as I studied Scripture, I wrote down one verse that I dwelled on for the next few months: "We are powerless against this mighty army that is about to attack us. We don't know what to do, and so we are looking to you for help" (2 Chronicles 20:12).

That's all the hope I had. A fraction of a verse stolen from a larger context, messily scribbled into a journal and a mite of hope that if I'd looked for God to help, he'd rescue my Ma and me. And he did. Not with wealth or healing but with peace, hope, and just enough provisions for each day. I found hope in that small verse; but the truth is, it's impossible to read the Scriptures without finding the many exhortations to be strong and full of hope. God is with *us*. *With* us.

HANGING ON TO HOPE

Hopelessness shouldn't be our normal state of affairs. A believer's soul can be anchored in hope. Does it make a lot of sense? No! Absolutely not, but there it is in Scripture screaming out to the poor, to the hopeless, to the addict: The kingdom of heaven is yours. It is yours!

Our hope is founded on the words of a God who cannot lie. *When we abandon hope, we express an unbelief in God.* If hope is the anchor of our soul, then giving up hope is a sign that our anchor has not been established deeply enough. There isn't anything on this earth so lacking or so broken that God cannot restore and redeem. When we declare ourselves too broken or lacking to do anything, we deny Jesus' power and the humility, hope, and faith available to us. Our hopeless scenarios may change very little, but the kingdom of heaven will not. When the poor are able to possess the kingdom of heaven—even in its not-so-completed state— they will find the courage and the hope necessary to survive this crazy, jacked-up life. Even the most hopeless among us.

POVERTY AND THE KINGDOM

Can we possess the kingdom of heaven here on earth and still live in poverty? Can it be simultaneous? After all, Jesus did not stutter. Could it be that Jesus does not always take away the crappy circumstances of our lives, but rather, gives hope in the midst of it? I cling to this, people. I cling. On my darkest days, I remember that I can still find myself in possession of spiritual rewards that far outweigh the temporary struggles I face today.

The hopeless, the poor, those in despair, and the powerless all have equal access to God. May the poor in spirit seek the Father to be filled. May we be like Jacob. May we freely admit, "I am poor; I am needy; and I need you, Lord." Embracing our need for God, through faith, hope, and humility is the foundational step for a happy soul and spirit anchored deeply.

Keep this truth close, and give it away to the poor among you. They will always be with us.

QUESTIONS

1. What is hope? Why is it important? How does it differ from faith?

Hope is something you are wishing for. And Faith is the strong hold that you have and can fell back on.

2. Why does Jesus say that people who are hopeless are happy? What does he mean?

- I have seen 3 world people that are happyer then we are in this country.
- people learn to live with what they have and not what they want.

3. Have you ever faced a seemingly hopeless situation? Was happiness a part of that experience for you? How do you view your experience in light of Matthew 5:3?

I was alway told growing-up be happy with what you have, there are people with less, also if god wanted you to have more he would give it.

4. What is the kingdom of heaven? Why does Jesus say that it belongs to the hopeless?

everyone and we are all hopeless

33

5. This section of Matthew is known as the Beatitudes. Some translations use the word *blessed* instead of *happy* in these verses. How are those words similar in meaning? How do they differ?

If you are blessed - you will be happy

if God is blessing you and you have a change in you everyone around you will see it.

6. How might Matthew 5:6 speak to someone who's facing poverty?

talking about someone who is seaching for God, and doing what God wants us to do.

7. How does Matthew 5:7 apply to the church and its response to those dealing with poverty?

show mercy - they will recieve mercy

Crop walk
Food Bank
clothing Closet

8. How can someone get a pure heart (Matthew 5:8)? Is it more
NO difficult to have a pure heart if you're wealthy? What about if you're poor? How does a person's response to poverty (whether first-hand poverty or someone else's) reflect the purity of his or her heart?

9. Is there a connection between peacemaking and reaching out to those struggling with poverty (Matthew 5:9)?

10. How can those who are facing poverty let their lights shine (Matthew 5:16)?

I think they undersand more and are more willing to give what they have

11. What is the link between spiritual poverty and material poverty? Imagine and describe scenarios where someone might be experiencing either, neither, or both.

Spiritual - the lack of understandy of God and what he wants from us.

material - is what we want from us (me) and can't have it.

12. What steps can we take to build hope in our lives? How do we grow spiritually rich?

I think we have to put our wants 2nd and put other people 1st.

My hope is everyone live free + happy with the Lord.

35

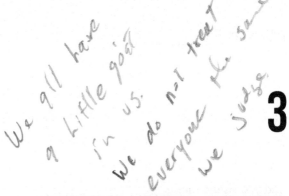

We all have a little god in us. We do not treat everyone the same we judge.

3

SHEEP AND GOATS
RESPONDING TO THE CRIES OF THE POOR

SCRIPTURE
PROVERBS 21:13; MATTHEW 25:31-46

PROVERBS 21:13

[13]Those who close their ears to the cries of the poor will themselves call out but receive no answer.

MATTHEW 25:31-46

[31]"Now when the Human One comes in his majesty and all his angels are with him, he will sit on his majestic throne. [32]All the nations will be gathered in front of him. He will separate them from each other, just as a shepherd separates the sheep from the goats. [33]He will put the sheep on his right side. But the goats he will put on his left.

[34]"Then the king will say to those on his right, 'Come, you who will receive good things from my Father. Inherit the kingdom that was

prepared for you before the world began. [35]I was hungry and you gave me food to eat. I was thirsty and you gave me a drink. I was a stranger and you welcomed me. [36]I was naked and you gave me clothes to wear. I was sick and you took care of me. I was in prison and you visited me.'

[37]"Then those who are righteous will reply to him, 'Lord, when did we see you hungry and feed you, or thirsty and give you a drink? [38]When did we see you as a stranger and welcome you, or naked and give you clothes to wear? [39]When did we see you sick or in prison and visit you?'

[40]"Then the king will reply to them, 'I assure you that when you have done it for one of the least of these brothers and sisters of mine, you have done it for me.'

[41]"Then he will say to those on his left, 'Get away from me, you who will receive terrible things. Go into the unending fire that has been prepared for the devil and his angels. [42]I was hungry and you didn't give me food to eat. I was thirsty and you didn't give me anything to drink. [43]I was a stranger and you didn't welcome me. I was naked and you didn't give me clothes to wear. I was sick and in prison, and you didn't visit me.'

[44]"Then they will reply, 'Lord, when did we see you hungry or thirsty or a stranger or naked or sick or in prison and didn't do anything to help you?' [45]Then he will answer, 'I assure you that when you haven't done it for one of the least of these, you

haven't done it for me.' [46]And they will go away into eternal punishment. But the righteous ones will go into eternal life.".

INSIGHT AND IDEAS

When I was 19, a thousand years ago, people listened to audiocassette tapes on a portable device called a Walkman®. In those olden days, my friend Natalie and I made a musical trade. She gave me a tape with a full live concert from Keith Green, while I gave her the sound-track tape to the Urbana 1996 Missions Conference. I was so astonished that anyone would trade a 180-minute tape for a mere one-hour album, that to this day, I feel I got the better end of the bargain.

Before this tape, I'd never heard of Keith Green or his music. Because of this general unfamiliarity, listening to him was truly refreshing. The depth of his lyrics and the emotion that poured out of him ministered deeply to my soul, in particular, the song "The Sheep and the Goats." In the song, he walks through Matthew 25:31-46, acting out each part set to a jittery, frenetic piano solo. I listen to that song over and over again. There's something in the way he represents Jesus' confrontational and loving voice, something in the way he pleads for forgiveness on behalf of the goats that brings the entire story to brilliant three-dimensional life. If you've never heard the song, may I suggest that you pause right here, head on over to YouTube, and watch him perform this powerful little song. I'll wait for you here.

See? Wasn't that amazing? God bless Keith Green. What Keith was able to emphasize without saying it was the dramatic culmination of an important talk Jesus had just had with his disciples on the Mount of Olives. He'd been using parables, when all of a sudden, he tells this straightforward story. No more ten maidens, talents, and tables. Now he's ready for the brass tacks.

Contextually, why wouldn't he be? It's easy to forget that this simple story is the preface to Jesus' Big Story. Jesus and his ragtag group of followers are merely days away from a final supper, a betrayal, an arrest, a torture, a death, and three long days of confusion. With rulers and kings plotting against Jesus at that very moment, for all intents and purposes, he is a goner. His crowds are gone, his friends are powerless nobodies, and here he is, bold as ever, declaring in verses 31-32a: "Now when the Human One comes in his majesty and all his angels are with him, he will sit on his majestic throne. All of the nations will be gathered in front of him."

WHAT, JESUS? WHAT?

He's clearly in no position to declare that his human self is coming back in majesty, with angels, thrones, tiaras, nations gathered, and such. The disciples must have thought that he was on crack. Yet this is how he begins his passionate call to love the least of our brothers and sisters. Jesus never ceases to be interesting.

DID JESUS REALLY JUST SAY THAT?

Let's take a deeper look at the connections Jesus has made. In his present state, Jesus has been little more than a three-year, semi-famous golden boy with no real positional power. He came to earth as a servant and will die with paupers. But now he's saying he's coming back—no such humility—complete with a picture of *all* people gathered *for him*. And in that power, he will divide up *all* of the people based solely on how they treated the poor. Really? Wow. This scenario should send off alarm bells to pay attention. Obviously, Jesus' words here are important.

TWO TYPES OF PEOPLE

According to Jesus, there are two types of people in this story: the sheep and the goats. He leaves no room for middle ground. Type 1, the sheep, meets the needs of all of the poor, no matter who they are. Their generosity is shown practically to the "least of these brothers and sisters of mine" (verse 40). Type 2, the goats, haven't lifted one of their pretty little fingers for anyone. The delineation here is important, because the sheep and the goats meet two very different ends.

THE GOATS

So who are these poor folks Jesus is speaking of? Not all commentators and biblical scholars agree, but many hold to the idea that Jesus was referring to caring for our fellow brothers and sisters of the faith. First John 4:20 states: "If anyone says, I love God, and hates a brother or sister, he is a liar, because the person who doesn't love a brother or sister who can be seen can't love God, who can't be seen."

True love for Jesus means that we will love the team of ragamuffins united in Christ all across our globe. It doesn't take a fortune or even a middle-class existence to care for the least of our brothers and sisters. Actually, what Jesus mentions here is quite simple: food, drink, welcome, clothes, and a prison visit or two. No one on earth could argue that those few things are too hard to do. No one, except, of course, the goats. The goats will ask, "Lord, when did we see you hungry or thirsty or a stranger or naked or sick or in prison and didn't do anything to help you?" (verse 44).

The implication is that these supposed Jesus-following goats saw the poor among them yet passed on the other side of the road. Jesus is saying that if you don't love them, you don't love him. If you don't love Jesus, or choose to love the poor through actionable items, you've got a punishment coming. Well, dang!

THE SHEEP

Not so for the sheep. Jesus gives mercy to the merciful. They get the full shebang: an inherited kingdom prepared for them since, well, the beginning of time. This is their inheritance, so to speak, bequeathed in Jesus' last will and testament. All of *that* for six nice deeds? Apparently. Yet, this list is not exhaustive. The six deeds are snapshots of particular needs met for the least of these. It's comforting for me to consider that *any nice deed I do* for the least of my brothers and sisters will beget similar mercy. Sometimes all I have time for is listening on the phone to a friend mourning the loss of her mother. When I can offer a meal or even a Facebook message of encouragement to a friend in need of kind words, I will. When I look around my community, what I see are endless needs among endlessly broken and precious human beings. You and I will never run out of opportunities to care for the "little" yet practical, basic needs of each every "least of these" in our respective communities.

It's refreshing to note the surprise of the sheep. They loved others in response to the love Jesus gave them, not for reward. Yet Jesus praises them, explaining in Matthew 25:40 that, "When you have done it for one of the least of these brothers and sisters of mine, you have done it for me." It's important to acknowledge that Jesus doesn't say, "when you have done it for a whole city of poor folk," or "when you have paid to build a school for the poor in South Africa," or "when you have fed every poor person in downtown Detroit. No, Jesus highlights that when you have done it for *one* of the least of his brothers and sisters, you have done it unto him. Shazam!

WHO ARE THE LEAST OF THESE?

It is interesting to broaden out the concept of "the least of these brothers and sisters of mine," beyond merely the financially poor. For example, in many countries today, Christians are heavily persecuted. Of course, it's easier to give to little African babies with bloated bellies and drippy noses when we can see the crystal clear image on our

Two fold to help other - BUT do iT with no pay back.

television screens, staring deep into our guilty eyes; but what about the Chinese pastor whose name or face we have never seen?

What about the prisoners? Prisons in America today are a multi-billion-dollar industry filled with invisible faces of hopelessness and trauma. It's hard to believe that our little weekly prayer meetings will make a difference for our brothers and sisters across the globe, but they will. And we ought to be willing to support these brothers and sisters through prayers, letters, financial and personal support with every resource available to us. It's the goats who allow themselves to overlook these types of needs. When your love for Jesus doesn't pull your heartstrings to love the least of our brothers and sisters, it's time to reevaluate your relationship with Christ. You just might be a goat.

THE PART NO ONE LIKES TO HEAR

Here's the troubling part of this passage. This is the part where Jesus gets eerily specific about an extremely harsh punishment. In Matthew 25:41, Jesus proclaims to the goats, "Get away from me, you who will receive terrible things. Go into the unending fire that has been prepared for the devil and his angels." The goats will receive terrible things. Unending fire. The devil will be there. Things really don't get much worse than this, folks. This reality? This is rock bottom.

Trust me, no one squirms more than *moi* at fire-and-brimstone preaching. And this is exactly what Jesus seems to be doing. In fact, if he were standing in the middle of Times Square giving this message, I'm sure he'd get run out of town, possibly hurt. Here's the thing: The context in which this story is told is part of a bigger narrative where Jesus has also given other specific, fire-and-brimstone-ish type of judgments. There are images of folks being cut into pieces, locked out, cast into outer darkness with weeping and gnashing of teeth and such. These are not sanitized judgments. These are hard-core consequences of a life lived outside of God's intentions, and it's legitimately scary.

It is unimaginable that Jesus would proclaim that anyone would receive "terrible things" in "unending fire," yet that is the punishment for failing to be our brother's and sister's keeper, for failing to do what could have been done and what ought to have been done when love for Jesus is shown practically in love for others. If I could save the life of my son Ransom by offering him one of my kidneys but I fail to do so because I'd rather overlook his need for my own selfish purposes, I am not showing concern for the least of these.

Jesus' public ministry comes to an end with this sobering story. I'd like to think of it as his final opus, the story that carries the most weight and impact. Thankfully for us, God's kingdom rules are simple; and those who choose to live by them will experience the joy of God's eternal kingdom.

QUESTIONS

1. What is the significance of "all the nations" being gathered before Jesus in Matthew 25:32?

Everyone will be judge.

2. Why does Jesus separate the "sheep" from the "goats" (Matthew 25:32)? Who are the sheep? Who are the goats?

Sheep is his follower
goat is devil Followers

3. Why, do you think, does Jesus identify so closely with the least of these in this passage?

Him + his followers was one of them that need the people.

4. What is noteworthy about Matthew 25:37-39 when compared to Matthew 25:44? What might these verses be saying about the conditions of the hearts and the motives of those on the left and those on the right?

5. What is the "unending fire that has been prepared for the devil and his angels" (Matthew 25:41)? Contrast this with the "kingdom that was prepared for you before the world began" (Matthew 25:34). Why doesn't Jesus say that the fire was prepared for the "goats" as well? *Hell*

6. What tension might this passage create when presented in light of the relationship between salvation, grace, and faith?

Treat everyone the same at no cost

7. What are the potential theological dangers of reading the Matthew 25 passage in isolation from the rest of Scripture?

8. How might Proverbs 21:13 be related to the concept of sowing and reaping?

9. How can we make sure that our motives are pure when we help the least of these?

10. What steps can we take to safeguard ourselves against becoming "goats"?

Lev Chapter 25
Deut 15 V–11

4

6 year
Work
7 year Take rea5
giving back to
the poor

THE FAST GOD CHOOSES
PRAYING TO HEAR THE CRIES OF THE POOR

SCRIPTURE
ISAIAH 58:1-12

[1]Shout loudly; don't hold back;
   raise your voice like a trumpet!
Announce to my people their crime,
   to the house of Jacob their sins.
[2]They seek me day after day,
   desiring knowledge of my ways
   like a nation that acted righteously,
   that didn't abandon their God.
They ask me for righteous judgments,
   wanting to be close to God.
[3]"Why do we fast and you don't see;
   why afflict ourselves and you don't notice?"
Yet on your fast day you do whatever you want,

and oppress all your workers.

⁴You quarrel and brawl, and then you fast;

you hit each other violently with your fists.

You shouldn't fast as you are doing today

if you want to make your voice heard on high.

⁵Is this the kind of fast I choose,

a day of self-affliction,

of bending one's head like a reed

and of lying down in mourning clothing and ashes?

Is this what you call a fast, a day acceptable to the LORD?

⁶Isn't this the fast I choose:

releasing wicked restraints, untying the ropes of a yoke,

setting free the mistreated,

and breaking every yoke?

⁷Isn't it sharing your bread with the hungry

and bringing the homeless poor into your house,

covering the naked when you see them,

and not hiding from your own family?

⁸Then your light

will break out like the dawn,

and you will be healed quickly.

Your own righteousness

will walk before you,

and the LORD's glory will be your rear guard.

⁹Then you will call,

and the LORD will answer;

you will cry for help, and God will say, "I'm here."

If you remove the yoke from among you,

    the finger-pointing, the wicked speech;

[10]if you open your heart to the hungry,

and provide abundantly for those who are afflicted,

your light will shine in the darkness,

and your gloom will be like the noon.

[11]The LORD will guide you continually

    and provide for you, even in parched places.

    He will rescue your bones.

You will be like a watered garden,

    like a spring of water that won't run dry.

[12]They will rebuild ancient ruins

    on your account;

    the foundations of generations past you will restore.

You will be called

    Mender of Broken Walls,

    Restorer of Livable Streets.

INSIGHT AND IDEAS

Going through the motions is, unfortunately, a life default for me. I have to drag my lazy self out of my emotional slumber for hearty wake-up calls at least biweekly. Going through the motions is easy-peasy. There's no challenge to it, no pushback—it's where the term "ignorance is bliss," came from. In our faith? It's a no-no. We don't move God by going through the motions. We don't move God by becoming modern-day Pharisees, so bound by our religious right-hood that we wouldn't know how to engage the Lord in meaningful ways if it hit us in the face.

In this passage, we come face-to-face with God's straightforward words that following religious rituals is far less than what was intended for us. What moves our Lord is a genuine compassion for the poor, the oppressed, and the helpless among us. In fact, it is within the context of a deep and intimate relationship with God that our desire to seek justice and to act compassionately will flourish.

God's heavy words to the recipients of these verses reveal how far from God's heart they were. Quick heart check: How far away from God's heart are *you*? Do you feel like the crappiest person to ever walk the planet when you read Isaiah 58? If you do, I'm not suggesting you stay there, but I do recommend that you allow the Holy Spirit's conviction to sit with you for a time.

TRYING TO MANIPULATE GOD

The folks this passage speaks of were clearly not interested in God's changing their heart and actions. They had no desire to let that conviction sit with them even momentarily. They wanted to fast *their* way. They wanted to perform their religious deeds *their* way, without dirtying themselves up with the muck of the homeless and hungry. While they longed for power, position, and possessions, God wanted to bless them with something entirely different, something that can't be bought with money or influence: compassion.

Not getting what they desired, they began to grumble to the Lord: "Why do we fast and you don't see; why afflict ourselves and you don't notice?" (verse 3). In other words, "God, what's up with that, yo?" I can understand that somewhat. Look, just like you and me, they did what they thought they had to do. They carried out their prescriptive religious activities. They fasted. They tried to humble themselves before the Lord. Was their fasting potentially thoughtless, with no real end, except gaining the favor of people? Perhaps. Perhaps it was all for show or spiritual manipulation. I get it. I wish that I didn't get it, but I do. I can recall times that I've tried with everything in me to manipulate God into providing a way of life for me that was ultimately completely selfish and self-focused. *Sigh.* In those low moments, my fasts, prayers, and actions revealed very little of the type of self-denial God is looking for.

Our childish manipulations do not impress God. When we try to fast and even repent in order to obtain something from God, we display the level of emptiness of our soul, along with our empty bellies. In Isaiah 58:4, God says, "You quarrel and brawl, and then you fast; you hit each other violently with your fists. You shouldn't fast as you are doing today if you want to make your voice heard on high." In other words, they may as well have prayed, "God, make us successful, oppressive, contentious jerks!" Then without seeing results, they fasted again to know why not. Not to grow closer to the Lord, but in fasts of zero humility, to acquire more. The focus is fully on them, while God is expecting their focus to be fully on others. Quite the opposite. Quite.

We know that these religious fasters were simultaneously fasting while exploiting others. They were fighting amongst themselves; they were hypocritical; they kept oppressed individuals among them; they refused to share with the hungry or house the homeless—yet they prayed for blessing.

Y'all, they prayed *for blessing*. How is that even possible? Their tomfoolery is reminiscent of American slavery when the awful practice was affirmed by the Christian religious majority of the day and was written into law and backed by a destructive use of Scripture. God wanted to bless Isaiah's listeners, and with so much more: healing, answered prayer, guidance, strength, joy, and more. Yet they chose something far less, which ultimately hurt not only them but those they could have served and loved. They fasted for blessing for themselves instead of obedience for themselves. What a loss!

THE COST OF DISOBEDIENCE

When believers who have resources to care for the poor, to free the prisoners, and house the homeless don't do so, who pays the most? The cost to the poor of our disobedience is astronomical. The Lord says through the prophet Isaiah in verse five, "Is this the kind of fast I choose, a day of self-affliction, of bending one's head like a reed and of lying down in mourning clothing and ashes? Is this what you call a fast, a day acceptable to the LORD?" In other words, we ought to have concern—actual concern—for those who need and long for liberation. The reason we should fast is not merely to check off our religious to-do list but for strength to do what we need to do to liberate.

Liberation itself is costly journey. When I read the newsletters of the work of the International Justice Mission, I am sobered at the dangerous, heart-breaking, soul-shaking work of those on the ground who are working to free men and women from the bondage of slavery. Thank God for them! Thank God for their willingness to make their life a fast in which God honors!

May I suggest a fast for you and me? Let us fast that we would open our eyes and our hearts clearly to the cries of the poor, that we would no longer hide from feelings of guilt, shame, or inadequacy that come along with a knowledge of the destitute. Let us fast for the homeless, the lost, the misplaced, and those in prison. Let us fast for the emotionally impoverished to be delivered from the bondage of oppressive spirits. Let us fast for those who are living under the weight of unhealthy interdependence on others and who need the grace to be set free.

> Isn't this the fast I choose:/releasing wicked restraints, untying the ropes of a yoke,/setting free the mistreated,/and breaking every yoke?/Isn't it sharing your bread/with the hungry/and bringing the homeless poor into your house,/covering the naked when you see them,/and not hiding from your own family? (Isaiah 58:6-7)

It doesn't get clearer than that, folks.

THE YOKE OF INJUSTICE

The image of breaking a yoke powerfully displays the complete destruction of oppression. If God's desires weren't for the complete annihilation of oppression he might have said something along the lines of, "Make the yoke a wee bit lighter for the oppressed to carry," or "Soften the blow of homeless a tiny little scooch." No, this image is a full picture of what God wants for creation: freedom. Freedom from all that binds us, starting with meeting our most basic needs: food, shelter, clothing, and proper treatment. We who have been freed to enjoy such freedoms ought to spread that freedom to others in an all-out war against injustice.

I would never sugarcoat the amount of effort it takes to rely on God's power enough to enact justice amidst our completely screwed up and systemic grievances against the poor. Yes, it's hard. Yet Scripture is clear: We are not to neglect this in any way, any shape, or any form. Our acknowledgement that every single thing we have belongs to the Lord will naturally lead us to share it generously. It ain't ours any old way.

The sort of fasting that God honors—to release the yoke of injustice—will change your heart, will make your compassion as soft and malleable as a designer stuffed teddy bear. God's desire is that each of us undergo this type of heart transformation. Each of us are to divide our individual daily bread with the hungry, not give them our half-eaten leftovers. If we have more than enough and our gifts are something we have little concern for, where is the sacrifice in that? We ought to allow our hearts the type of dramatic transformation that allows for us to *actually* deny ourselves something. We are to provide homes for those who have none, supply clothing for those who haven't a thread, and address the needs of our relatives by acknowledging their situations and taking care of them.

SHARING THE BLESSING

I have struggled with this tremendously. I have a relative who spent many years in prison and since his release has struggled to hold down a job and secure housing. Every now and then when he requests money, I give it to him as I'm able; but there's always a little voice in my head wondering if I'm enabling him, or if I'm being bamboozled and used. And Lord Jesus, why isn't he on his feet yet?

Here's the deal. He's been hungry and he's been homeless, and I've helped. I didn't help because I was supposed to; I helped because I've never let my doubts trump my compassion for his condition. Maybe I have enabled him at times. Maybe he does fall back on me too quickly. I'd rather err on the side of helping him through his hard times, with a possible risk of being used rather than see him miss even one meal.

Having grown up poor, my family and I understand the absolute need to rely on others, to look to God, and to hope that enough people who have experienced God's compassion will extend it to us. As a little girl, seeing people come along side to feed and clothe me in my desperate times of need was all the outward evidence of a good and loving God that I needed. I identify strongly with the hungry and naked. My faith would lack complete integrity if I didn't share all that I had with my relative or others who need it.

God's people are to share with those who lack the basic needs of life. Those who know the compassionate blessing of God in their own lives ought to extend it to others. Thankfully, by God's grace, I'm more concerned with others than with God's blessing me for my small sacrifices. Yet what I've noticed is that the more I give generously, the more kindness, compassion, and generosity grows in my heart. That in and of itself has been a wonderful gift—an outpouring of the Holy Spirit in unexpected but welcome ways.

I encourage you to go on a good old fast. Fast for a heart change; fast for the end of injustice. Fast for the kidnapped Nigerian girls. Fast for the homeless of your city. Fasting is a lot more than not eating. It's allowing ourselves to be transformed and used in ways that truly please God and to trust God to fill us with things that are greater and more fulfilling than anything we think we desire.

May God so bless your fast that you hear clearly the cries of the poor!

QUESTIONS

1. What does Isaiah 58 have to say about sincerity when it comes to prayer, fasting, and worship?

2. What do verses 3 and 4 seem to be saying about relying on our desire to know God? Why isn't this enough to get God's attention?

3. Compare and contrast the ideas in this Scripture passage with James 2:26: "As the lifeless body is dead, so faith without actions is dead."

4. What are the yokes of bondage and oppression that need to be broken in our culture today (Isaiah 58:6)? What can you do to contribute to breaking those yokes?

5. In what ways might we sometimes block the answers to our own prayers?

6. How do the provisions we receive from God connect to us helping to provide for those who need help (Isaiah 58:10-11)?

7. How can we guard against attempting to manipulate God when we fast and pray?

8. How does fasting transform us? How does it produce spiritual dividends that might affect our future praying and fasting?

9. What is the connection between fasting and repentance?

10. What are areas of your life that need to be transformed by prayer and fasting? What about in the lives of the people around you?

Check out Grace Biskie's
other title in the Converge series!

Kingdom Building
9781426771576, Print
9781426771699, eBook

 Abingdon Press™

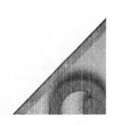

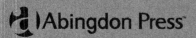

CPSIA information can be obtained at www.ICGtesting.com
Printed in the USA
LVOW04s1238050515

437202LV00019BA/253/P

9 781426 795558